SUPER SKATEBOARDING™

SKATEBOARDING
TODAY AND TOMORROW

rosen publishing's
rosen central®

New York

HEATHER HASAN

To my nephew, Gabriel, with love

Published in 2009 by The Rosen Publishing Group, Inc.
29 East 21st Street, New York, NY 10010

Library of Congress Cataloging-in-Publication Data

Hasan, Heather.
Skateboarding today and tomorrow / Heather Hasan.—1st ed.
    p. cm.—(Super skateboarding)
Includes bibliographical references.
ISBN-13: 978-1-4358-5049-1 (library binding)
ISBN-13: 978-1-4358-5393-5 (pbk)
ISBN-13: 978-1-4358-5399-7 (6 pack)
1. Skateboarding—History. I. Title.
GV859.8.H37 2009
796.22—dc22

                                                    2008018023

Manufactured in the United States of America

On the cover: A skateboarder performs a frontside air in a concrete pool.

CONTENTS

MAR 0 9 2010

INTRODUCTION

Today, there are more than fifty million skateboarders in the world. They all share a love for the freedom and excitement that skateboarding provides.

Skateboarding, or skating, is a sport that involves doing tricks on a specially designed wooden board with four wheels. The sport of skateboarding has experienced many changes since kids first began nailing roller skates to the bottom of wooden planks in the early 1900s. As skateboarding has changed, the type of skating that is popular has shifted. The image of skateboarders has also changed. The tricks performed by skateboarders have changed and advanced throughout the years. The equipment for skateboarding has become more specialized and advanced.

Though the sport has changed a lot, skateboarding today is more popular than ever. There are more than fifty million skateboarders in the world today. These skateboarders share a love for the freedom and thrill that skateboarding gives them. This book explores the current trends and changes occurring in the world of skateboarding. It will look at the top skaters, the latest equipment, and the current tricks and skating competitions.

CHAPTER ONE

TOP SKATERS

The sport of skateboarding is always changing and growing. It is the skaters who keep the sport interesting. They are always trying new moves and inventing new tricks. In the world of skateboarding, skaters that have been around for a long time are often as popular as newcomers to the sport. Some of the most popular skaters today are Tony Hawk, Rodney Mullen, Bucky Lasek, and Ryan Sheckler.

Tony Hawk

When Tony Hawk was nine years old, his brother gave him his first skateboard. This changed his life. By the age of twelve, Hawk was sponsored by Dogtown Skateboards. At age sixteen, he was a professional skateboarder. By the time he was seventeen, Hawk was considered the best skateboarder in the world. Though he retired in 1999, Hawk is still quite active in the skateboarding world.

Though he no longer skates competitively, Hawk still skates almost every day. He is always coming up with new tricks, and he shows off these new tricks at the public demos he does each year. Hawk is still one of the best skateboarders in the world. In fact, he was recently voted the best vert skater in *Transworld Skateboarding* magazine (vert skateboarding involves riding up and down a vertical half-pipe).

Here, Tony Hawk is performing at the Laureus Beach Festival in Estoril, Portugal. The Laureus Beach Festival includes surfing, bodyboarding, windsurfing, kitesurfing, kiteflying, and skateboarding.

Shortly before he retired, Hawk became the first skater to land a 900 (two-and-a-half midair spins). The 900 is among the tricks he invented. Others include the 540 ollie, the 540 kickflip, and the 720 varial.

In 2002, Hawk started the Boom Boom HuckJam. This popular thirty-city tour features the best skateboarders, BMX bike riders, and motocross riders. They perform while punk and hip-hop music play in the background. Since its start, the Boom Boom HuckJam has sold out every year. Hawk also has a clothing line called Hawk Clothing. It includes clothes and footwear that is sold only at Kohl's stores.

Hawk even has a roller coaster named after him. Six Flags amusement parks in Texas, Missouri, and California currently have the skateboarding-themed roller coaster Tony Hawk's Big Spin.

He also has his own computer and video game series. The series began in 1999, with *Tony Hawk's Pro Skater*. This video game was so popular that other games soon followed. *Tony Hawk's Proving Ground* was released in 2007. Players are able to completely customize their skaters. They are also able to play online and skate with other players.

In 1992, Hawk started a skateboard company called Birdhouse Skateboards. Birdhouse makes decks, wheels, clothing, and accessories. The company also makes skateboarding videos. Birdhouse's first video, *The End*, was released in 1998. The company's most featured video, *The Beginning*, was released in 2007. This video shows Hawk and other riders, including his son Riley, doing some exciting and intense skateboarding.

Rodney Mullen

Rodney Mullen is known as the "King of Freestyle." Freestyle skateboarding is the oldest style of skateboarding. Freestyle was popular on and off from the 1960s to the 1990s. It involves doing technical street tricks on a smaller board. A freestyle skater needs only a flat surface to perform. Early freestyle involved choreographing skateboarding to music. While performing, a freestyle skater finds creative ways to go from trick to trick.

Freestyle skating changed a lot in the 1980s, when ollies and ollie-based flip tricks were introduced. The ollie involves a rider pushing off the back foot on the board, springing into a jump, and bringing his or her knees up. Around the time that the ollie was introduced, street skateboarding emerged from freestyle skating. Street skating involves the use of obstacles that are found in urban, or city, environments. These include things such as stairs, handrails, and curbs. Mullen switched from freestyle skating to street skating in the early 1990s. He combined his awesome freestyle tricks with street skating. Though he did not invent the ollie, Rodney Mullen is responsible for inventing the street ollie. Most of the ollies and flip tricks Mullen invented in the 1980s are still done regularly in modern, new-school street and vertical skateboarding. Some of these tricks include the flatground ollie, the heelflip, the kickflip, the 360 flip, and the ollie impossible.

Rodney Mullen is a major force in the world of street skating. Many tricks Mullen invented formed the foundation of skateboarding today.

In 2003, Mullen was voted the all-time best action sports athlete by the Extreme Sports Channel's *Legends of the Extreme* countdown. He is described as having more grace and coordination than any other skateboarder. In 2004, Mullen wrote his autobiography, *The Mutt: How to Skateboard and Not Kill Yourself*. He also works for Dwindle Distribution, the world's largest skateboard manufacturer. He directs the production of skateboard decks. Mullen still continues to skate. He has also appeared in many video games, including *Tony Hawk's Proving Ground*.

Bucky Lasek

Bucky Lasek is a vert skater. He began skateboarding in 1984, at the age of twelve. Lasek turned pro six years later, in 1990. In the mid-1990s, vert skating became part of the X Games, a popular extreme sports competition. Lasek soon became one of the most popular and recognizable skaters. Today, he is considered one of the most creative and consistent vert skaters in the business.

Lasek skates for hours every day and has invented many tricks. Many of the tricks he masters are thought of by other skaters as too difficult to try during competition. Lasek regularly lands them without mistake, however. Some of the tricks that Lasek is known for include the heelflip frontside gay twist and the switch frontside 540. He is thought of as an inventive and aggressive skater. He is one of only two skaters that do a heelflip frontside invert (flipping the board into an invert). He is also the only skateboarder that does a 720 on the vert, landing backward (forward-to-fakie 720).

Lasek has won twelve X Games medals, including seven gold medals. He has also had many Slam City Jam skateboarding championship victories. Lasek even has a couple of gold medals from the Gravity Games, another popular skateboarding competition. He has appeared in movies such as *Grind and Haggard: The Movie* and in television shows such as *Punk'd*, *Cribs*, and *MADtv*. He was also a character in the video game *Tony Hawk's Pro Skater*. In 2004, Bucky Lasek became the first action sports athlete to be on the cover of *ESPN* magazine.

Ryan Sheckler

Ryan Sheckler stepped on his first skateboard at the age of eighteen months. He joined the California Amateur Skateboarding League (CASL). The CASL is an organization that gives young skaters a safe place to practice and compete. Sheckler won the CASL champion-ships in 1996 (at the age of seven) and 1997 (at the age of eight).

Here, Bucky Lasek is doing an invert during the Mountain Dew National Championship in New Jersey.

In 2003, at the age of thirteen, Sheckler turned pro. That same year, he won first place in several skateboarding competitions, including the X Games, the Gravity Games, Slam City Jam, and the Vans Triple Crown. Since turning pro, Sheckler has earned many skateboarding titles, including National Street Champion and World Street Champion.

In 2005, he took the overall skateboard park title at the Dew Action Sports Tour. Sheckler also claimed the Dew Action Sports Tour title in both 2006 and 2007. He has developed his own trick called

Ryan Sheckler is one of the sport's most innovative skaters, which he proved at the Los Angeles X Games street finals.

the Sheck-lair, which is an indy kickflip flyout. In 2007, he starred in an MTV reality series about his life called *The Life of Ryan*. The show was so popular, especially among young girls, that it is scheduled for another season. Sheckler also has his own shoe and clothing line, called Sheckler Merch.

Backside Grind

1. Approach the rail with moderate speed.
2. Spot your landing area. Once you ollie, you won't be able to see where you will land.
3. Ollie and spin 90 degrees, keeping your knees bent and your feet shoulder-width apart.
4. Land in-between the wheels with your back to the landing area.
5. As you come to the end of your grind, turn your shoulders with the board as you come off the edge.
6. Roll away.

CHAPTER TWO

THE EQUIPMENT

Skateboarding does not require a lot of equipment. It mainly just requires a rider and his or her board. However, a smart skateboarder will also use protective gear to avoid injury. Many skateboarders use knee and elbow pads, wrist guards, and a helmet. In fact, helmets are required by law in many areas. Safety equipment is important, especially for beginners. Protective gear allows experienced riders to try new tricks without fear of injury. Most pads are made of foam that is covered by plastic. The type of skateboarding shoe a rider wears can also add to the protection and the quality of ride a skateboarder gets.

Skateboard Shoes

As unbelievable as it sounds, the earliest skateboarders often did not wear shoes when they were skating. The first skateboarding shoes were Vans, which came out in 1966. Today, advanced technology is used to create shoes with increased grip, cushioning, and durability. In an effort to make better skate shoes, different mixes of rubbers, vinyls, polyurethanes (synthetic plastics), and gels are tried. Ideas have also been borrowed from other sports shoes. It is important that skateboarding shoes are made well in order to prevent injury. If the edges of shoe soles are not designed well or if an air bubble in the shoe bursts, a rider can suffer an ankle or heel injury. Skateboarding shoes should also be comfortable and have flexible soles. Some brands of popular skateboarding shoes today are Vans, Fallen Footwear, and Globe.

Fallen Footwear makes quality shoes that are unique and durable. They are also planet-friendly because they do not contain any animal products. Today, many skate shoe companies have models that are named after professional skateboarders. Fallen Footwear is owned by professional skateboarder Jamie Thomas.

Vans have been around for a long time, so the company has had

Skateboarders need shoes that are comfortable and have flexible soles. These shoes should also have soles that grip the board well.

lots of time to improve upon the design of the shoes. Two models of Vans that are often used by skateboarders are Geoff Rowley's Rowley XL2s and Dustin Dollin's No Skools. Both Rowley and Dollin are professional skateboarders. Rowley XL2s are made of leather and suede and have strong, puffy tongues. They are strangely light and have waffle soles that grip very well. Dustin Dollin's No Skools are made of suede and leather. They are strong, and the extra padding in their tongues and heel collars add comfort. The No Skools also have punk screen printing on the canvas side panels of the shoes and on their tongues to add style.

These boards are by Lib Technologies. The board on the left has a wooden bottom, while the one on the right is made with plastihide.

Globe is an Australian skateboarding shoe company. Many skateboarders enjoy the quality of these shoes and their inventive, modern features. Globe makes models like Vagrant and Finale. Vagrant shoes have a pre-worn style but are built to last. Finales have a more sporty look.

Skateboard Decks

Of course, the type of skateboard that a skater rides is very important. A skateboard has three parts: the deck (the main part of the board); the wheels; and the trucks, which connect the wheels to the board and allow it to turn. The deck is easily the most important part of the skateboard. Skateboard decks come in all kinds of shapes and sizes. The deck that a skateboarder chooses can greatly affect the way he or she skates. Skateboarders should choose decks that meet their particular needs. Today, most decks are between 7.5 and 8 inches (19.05–20.32 centimeters) wide. The lengths of skateboard decks are usually between 31 and 32.5 inches (78.74–82.55 cm). Smaller skateboards are often easier to control. Therefore, they are better for doing flip tricks. Wider boards are usually easier to carve (create big, deep turns) with.

Early skateboards were simply made from wood. In 1964, skateboard companies came to the realization that laminating the decks, or covering them with a thin sheet of protective material, made them more flexible. All skateboards today have this kind of flexibility to some extent.

In the 1970s, people began laminating decks entirely with maple. Maple is still used to laminate boards. Most skateboards today are made of seven-ply maple. This means that seven layers of maple wood are glued together. This seems to give the decks the best combination of strength, low weight, and flexibility.

Some skateboard companies, such as Mervin Manufacturing, are trying new constructions for skateboard decks. Mervin

Here, a skateboard maker adds a layer of magnesium oxide to a board. Magnesium oxide is about twice as strong as traditional fiberglass.

Manufacturing uses aspen wood instead of maple. Aspen is much lighter than maple. Though aspen is not as tough as maple, it is very break-resistant. Also, instead of making its boards seven-ply, Mervin Manufacturing uses only three layers of wood. Less wood and less glue also makes for a lighter board.

The company includes other features on its decks for added strength and board protection. These include a layer of birchwood around the board for added strength, internal polyethylene tip and tail protectors, a layer of fiberglass for extra strength, and a layer of graphite for a rigid pop.

Skateboard Wheels and Trucks

In 1973, urethane skateboard wheels replaced the metal and clay wheels that had been used. Today, all skateboard wheels are made of urethane, a durable plastic. It lasts long and does not lose its shape. Urethane wheels allow skateboarders to ride on any type of surface. However, they do have a tendency to slip when wet. New types of urethane are always being developed, so the construction of skateboard wheels is always improving.

Another part of the wheel, the bearings, has greatly improved through the years. The bearings keep the skateboard wheels spinning smoothly. Better bearing construction and urethane wheels allow skateboarders to go faster and jump higher, which means they can try more exciting tricks. Skateboard wheels come in a variety of sizes and have different degrees of hardness. Larger wheels roll faster and move over cracks in the pavement more easily. Smaller wheels are lighter and bring the board closer to the ground, giving the rider a smoother ride. Modern street skaters that like to do flip tricks usually prefer smaller, harder wheels. Vert skaters, on the other hand, usually prefer larger, harder wheels.

Trucks are the metal parts that hold the wheel to the skateboard deck. Materials such as plastic, brass, magnesium, and steel have all been used to make skateboard trucks. However, most manufacturers now use aluminum alloys, mixtures of aluminum and other metals.

Today, skateboard trucks need to be strong and light. Aluminum alloy trucks are ideal because they are both extremely strong and light. Many different companies make skateboard trucks. Some of these companies have tried to make their trucks lighter, while others focus on durability. Several advances in the design of trucks have been made in the last few years. One company that produces trucks is Tensor Trucks.

TENSOR

THE NEW LO TRUCK

LOWER KINGPIN, QUICKER TURN AND NEW COLORS

Tensor Trucks is a company that was founded by professional skateboarder Rodney Mullen. Tensor released an all-metal truck that was praised for being the lightest. Later, Tensor released a superlight truck made of magnesium.

This company offers trucks that have plastic grind plates. The grind plate protects the frame of the skateboard. This design helps when a skater is doing nose slides (sliding on the front of the board) and tail slides (sliding on the back of the board).

Another company, Phantom Trucks, offers built-in shock pads on the bottom of its trucks. They reduce the stress from the trucks to the board. One other company, Softtrucks, introduced practice trucks. These give the skateboarder the feel of regular trucks without the rolling action of wheels. They are designed specifically for practicing technical tricks.

Axel Stall

1. Approach the ramp with just the right amount of speed.
2. Spot your landing area.
3. Do half a kickturn right before you hit the coping and get your back trucks to connect.
4. Turn your backside to allow the front truck onto the coping.
5. When you are ready to come out of the stall, do another half kickturn.
6. Bend your knees and ride straight down.

CHAPTER THREE

THE TRICKS

Learning and mastering new tricks are goals of many skateboarders. Skaters do tricks on sidewalks, railings, half-pipes, ramps, and bowls. To do most tricks, skaters must first learn to ollie. The ollie is basically jumping with the skateboard. To ollie, a skater puts the front foot in the middle of the skateboard. The skater then stomps on the tail of the skateboard with the back foot. This is called popping off. The skater then slides the front foot farther up the board. As he or she flies through the air, the skateboard stays under the skater's feet. The ollie is the basic building block for almost all other skating tricks. It is impossible to list all of the new tricks that are out there. New tricks are constantly being invented. This keeps the sport of skateboarding interesting and exciting. Some categories of tricks include flip tricks, aerial tricks, and slides and grinds.

Flip Tricks

Flip tricks are a very important part of street skating. Flip tricks are any tricks where the skateboard flips or spins in the air. All of these tricks start with the ollie. Two common flip tricks are the kickflip and the pop shove-it. A kickflip turns the skateboard side-over-side under the skater. To do a kickflip, a skater brings his or her feet toward the center of the skateboard. The skater then places the toes of the front foot close to the backside rail of the skateboard deck. The skater then jumps up and quickly flips the board with his or her toes. Once the board is right side up, the skater can put both feet on it and land.

The pop shove-it spins the skateboard around in a half or full turn. The skater starts with an ollie. As the skater stomps down on the backside of the board, he or she also uses a foot to start the board spinning. The skater then gets his or her feet back on the board and lands.

Here, a sixteen-year-old skateboarder attempts to do an ollie on one of the obstacles at a skate park in Florida.

Aerials

Aerial tricks are performed while skaters are in the air. These are some of the most exciting tricks in skateboarding. Aerials are usually performed on half-pipes, on quarter-pipes that have a vertical section, or in pools. Aerials usually combine rotation (spinning) and different kinds of grabs. Spinning in the air is a big part of aerials. Spins are named for how many degrees the board turns. If a rider spins completely around (360 degrees), it is called a 360. If a skater spins only halfway around, it is called a 180. Right now, spins go as high as the 900. This involves spinning around two and a half times in the air.

There are endless numbers of grab tricks. They are called grab tricks because the skater grabs a part of the board with one or both hands while in the air. Some basic grabs include the mute, the indy, and the melon. The mute is done by grabbing the frontside (or toeside) of the deck with the front hand. The indy is done by grabbing the frontside of the deck with the back hand. The melon is done by grabbing the backside (or heelside) of the deck with the front hand. Skaters can

The World's Largest Skate Ramp

The largest skateboard ramp can be found on a twelve-acre farm north of San Diego, California. The Mega Ramp (as it is called) is longer than a football field and is as tall as an eight-story building. It belongs to professional skateboarder Bob Burnquist. Burnquist turned professional in 1990 at the age of fourteen. He has placed first in many Slam City Jam contests in the vert category. He has also won several gold medals in the X Games. Burnquist has been featured in many of Tony Hawk's video games. Burnquist's giant ramp was built in his backyard and cost $280,000. Speeds of 55 miles per hour (88.5 kilometers per hour) can be reached while riding Burnquist's ramp. During the ride, skaters are also launched across a 70-foot (21.3 meters) gap. Burnquist is described as a daredevil. During competitions, he is known for trying moves that no one else would dare to try.

Here, Bucky Lasek does a grab while competing in the Globe World Cup in Australia. He won the overall title.

make grabs as difficult as they want. They can add kicks or leg tucks, or can take the board out from under the body. The rocket air is done by grabbing the nose of the skateboard with both hands while placing both feet on the tail of the board.

Slides and Grinds

Slides and grinds are popular moves. To slide and grind, a skater must first ollie up onto some type of obstacle. In the late 1990s and early 2000s, skateboarders used traditional obstacles, such as ledges, rails, stairs, and curbs. Today, skateboarders slide and grind on more unusual things.

Slides and grinds are popular moves. The possibilities for what skaters can slide and grind on are endless. Here, a skater is using a bench.

They skate on random banks and oddly shaped structures. Skaters like Daewon Song are always looking for unique spots to skate. Song skates anything from benches and pools to rock formations, waterfalls, and the tops of cement buildings.

To slide, a skater drags the deck of the skateboard along the obstacle. To grind, the skater drags one or both of the trucks along the obstacle. There are all kinds of slides and grinds. They are usually named either for the part of the board that is touching the obstacle or for the type of obstacle being used. One of the most common types of grinds is the

50-50 grind. This involves the rider grinding equally on both trucks. A nose grind involves grinding on just the front truck. To do a nose slide, just the very front part of the deck comes into contact with the obstacle.

Combination Tricks

Many types of tricks can be combined to form new tricks. Finding new combinations is what keeps skateboarding new and exciting. Professional skaters combine two or more tricks into one new move. Some of the moves that were seen in the 2007 AST Dew Tour were the backside 540, the frontside 540 rodeo, and the heelflip frontside gay twist. A backside 540 is done by riding up the transition, grabbing the board on the heelside with the front hand, turning backside (toward the skater's toes), and landing forward. The frontside 540 rodeo is when the rider turns frontside (toward the heels) 180 degrees while completing an inverted (upside-down) 360, for a total of 540. A gay twist is a fakie (riding backward) to 360 while grabbing mute. The heelflip frontside gay twist is a variation of this where the board is spun with a forward kick from the front heel. During competitions, skateboarders are judged mainly on the difficulty and success of such tricks.

Backside Rock-and-Roll

1. Ride up the ramp.
2. At the top of the ramp, lift your front trucks over the coping.
3. Rest the bottom of the deck on the lip.
4. Twist your upper body and raise the front wheels.
5. Pivot 180 degrees on your back wheels and complete the kickturn.
6. Ride down the ramp.

1

2

3

4

5

6

CHAPTER FOUR

THE COMPETITIONS

Many skateboarders have become famous after competing in professional competitions like the Gravity Games and the X Games. Competitions usually feature new tricks. For competitions, skaters come up with a series of tricks, called a routine or run. The World Cup of Skateboarding (WCS) is an international skateboarding federation that organizes the World Championships of Skateboarding series. This takes place around the world. It also organizes several other skateboarding contests. Some of the contests it oversees are the X Games, the Gravity Games, the AST Dew Tour, and the Grand Slam of Pro Skateboarding.

X Games

The X Games is an annual contest for extreme action sports. It features sports like skateboarding, surfing, and motocross in the summer and snowboarding, skiing, and snowmobiling in the winter. The Winter X Games are held each year in January or February. The Summer X Games are held each August.

The X Games were started in 1995 by the ESPN network. Thanks to the X Games, skateboarding entered the world of TV. The games are shown live on ESPN and ABC television. The first X Games event was held in Newport, Rhode Island, and was called the Extreme Games.

Here, professional skateboarder Andy Macdonald is competing in the Skateboard Vert Men's Final during the ESPN X Games. Six disciplines of skateboard competitions are featured at the X Games.

Since that time, it has been known as the X Games. The competitors of the X Games do their best to try to win gold, silver, or bronze medals. Winners also receive prize money.

Gravity Games

The Gravity Games began in 1997. The competition is partially owned by NBC Sports. The Gravity Games is a multisport competition. It features extreme sports such as skateboarding, motocross, and wake-boarding during the summer, and snowboarding during the winter. The

This outdoor vert ramp in Woodward, PA, was used in the Gravity Games, which feature bikers and skaters soaring off of ramps like this.

street skateboarding competition involves no set routines. Riders exhibit their best moves on boxes, rails, and quarter-pipes. Skaters are judged mainly on creativity. During the vert competition, skaters have a limited amount of time to prove their skills on huge half-pipes. Along with the extreme sports, many musical groups also perform at the event. Many of the same skaters that participate in the X Games also compete in the Gravity Games.

AST Dew Tour

The AST Dew Tour is owned by NBC Universal. It is a sports tour that lasts an entire season. It consists of five multisport events. Included in the tour are skateboarding (vert and park), BMX motocross (vert, park, and dirt), and freestyle motocross. The points from all of these events are added up throughout the season. At the end of the season, the winners are awarded the Dew Cup. There is also a monetary prize.

The park-style skateboarding competitions allow skaters to show their technical skills as well as their ability to "go big." The course combines ledges and rails with park obstacles. The judges look for a variety of tricks. In the vert skateboarding competitions, the contestants have a certain amount of time to put together their best run on an 80-foot (24.3 meter) half-pipe. The skaters are judged on the height, flow, and difficulty of the tricks. In 2007, Ryan Sheckler won in the park skateboarding category, while Shaun White won for vert skateboarding.

Grand Slam of Pro Skateboarding

The Grand Slam of Pro Skateboarding is a new competition, starting in 2008. It consists of four international competitions for street and vert skating. This will become the new WCS point series. The competitions involved will be the Rio Vert Jam and Slam City Jam, the World Skateboarding Championships, the Mystic Sk8 Cup, and the Maloof Money Cup. The decision was made to make these competitions for skateboarding only. The WCS hopes that this will bring more value and respect to the events. It is also hoped that it will attract the top professional skaters.

Here, Shaun White competes in the AST Dew Tour Skateboard Vert Finals at the Rose Garden. He won in the vert skateboarding category.

Skateboarding and the Olympics

Skateboarding could possibly be involved in the 2012 Olympic Games in London, England. The International Olympic Committee will most likely have made its decision by 2009. If skateboarding makes it into

Is Vert Skating Dead?

ESPN seems to think that vert skating is dead. It announced that as of 2008, vert will no longer be a part of the X Games. Skating disciplines have always flowed in and out of popularity. It looks like it is vert skateboarding that is now out. Vert's TV ratings on ESPN have gone down over the last few years. A majority of skateboarders today consider themselves street, or park, skaters. Of the four thousand skate parks worldwide, there are only a few dozen vert ramps still standing. Most of these are in California. To reflect the new trend, the Summer X Games will now feature a new discipline, the SuperPark.

the Olympics, it will join two other extreme sports. Snowboarding joined the Winter Olympics in 1998 and BMX biking was scheduled to make its first Olympic appearance in the 2008 Summer Games in Beijing.

It is thought that adding skateboarding to the Olympics will attract younger people. Snowboarding received very high ratings on NBC in the 2006 Winter Olympics. Many skateboarders feel that joining the Olympics would make skateboarding an accepted sport and lead to more community support. However, there are others who feel that being part of the Olympics might have a negative impact on the sport. They feel it might lead to constrictive rules.

Frontside Smith Grind

1. Get some speed. The faster you go, the longer you will be able to grind.
2. Ollie up onto the coping.
3. Land so that your back trucks are grinding and the rail of the board is rubbing the edge, while your front trucks hang over the grinding surface.
4. When done grinding, give your tail a slight pop.
5. Land back on all four wheels.
6. Ride away.

CHAPTER FIVE

TRENDS IN SKATEBOARDING

Skateboarding is about being free, riding in whatever way is desired, and being able to invent an endless number of tricks. Skateboarding was first tied to the culture of surfing. In the late 1990s, a new kind of skateboarder appeared: the "punker." Punk music expressed skaters' desire for freedom and independence. However, skaters are not just "punkers." Many new trends can be seen today. At a skate park, one can find a variety of different types of people. There may be some punkers, but there are also preppies, Goths, and others. There are also likely to be female skaters there. What all of these people share is a love for the sport of skateboarding.

Moving Out of the Suburbs

According to the *New York Times*, more and more skaters are from big cities like New York. In part, this new trend is due to how skateboarders have gotten into urban styles. In the past, many big-city teens may have had a negative view of skateboarding. They saw it as something foreign that would sometimes trickle out of the suburbs. Skateboarding is now seen as a sport for everyone.

The increase in city skating can also be explained by the shift in popularity from ramp-based vert skating to street skating. Street, or park, skating lends itself to urban areas. Skaters are able to make use of city structures such as curbs, stairways, and railings. However, some of skateboarding's most successful skaters have recognized the need for skate parks in urban areas.

Tony Hawk has raised money for more than three hundred skate parks in low-income areas. In areas where skate parks have been built, they are reportedly used more than any other sporting facility, including tennis courts, basketball courts, and baseball fields.

Going "Old School"

Many of today's skaters are going "old school." This means that they are borrowing from the past and making it work for them today. Freestyle skating was popular from about the 1960s to the 1990s. Now, freestyle skateboarding is considered old-school skating. The "anything goes" philosophy of freestyle skateboarding appeals to skaters today because it gives them the freedom to explore new tricks. The skateboarder can decide upon the difficulty, style, and creativity of his or her tricks.

Recently, a number of professional skateboarders have been performing a lot of old-school tricks, such as wallrides and no-complys. Wall rides involve skating up a vertical wall. No-complys are done by placing the rear foot on the tail, then placing the front foot on the ground and popping the board into the air.

Another interesting turn in skateboarding is the revived popularity of pool skating. Vert skating actually began in the 1960s in drained swimming pools. Pool skating really gained popularity toward the end of 1970. It once again became popular in 2000, and it continues to be featured in skate videos.

Female Skateboarders

Elissa Steamer is one of the world's top female skateboarders and a pioneering figure in the sport. She's placed first in the Los Angeles X Games.

Skateboarding has always been a male-dominated sport. In the early years of skateboarding, few female skateboarders were well known. The 1990s saw an advancement in all women's sports, including skateboarding. More women skaters started to emerge. Female skaters like Elissa Steamer and Cara-Beth Burnside brought skateboarding to a new level. Steamer turned pro in 1998. She won the first women's street competition at Slam City Jam in British Columbia. She was voted the best female skater in the world in both 2003 and 2004 by *Check It Out* magazine. She has also appeared as a character in five of Tony Hawk's skateboarding video games.

Burnside started competing professionally against men in 1991. Throughout her skateboarding career, Burnside has won two gold medals in the X Games, five Vans Triple Crown titles, and four All Girls Skate Jam titles. The All Girls Skate Jam competition began in 1996. It is the only skateboarding competition that is exclusively for girls of all ages and abilities. It started out as a yearly national event, but, because of its popularity, the All Girl Skate Jam is now an international event. At the age of thirty-five, Burnside was named Female Skateboarder of the Year by *Transworld Skateboarding* magazine. In 2004, she was named

Female Vert Skater of the Year by World Cup Skating. She now serves as president of the Alliance. The Alliance is a nonprofit association for professional women skateboarders. Steamer and Burnside were pioneers for female skateboarding but also continue to play a large part in it.

Women continue to thrive in the world of skateboarding, with female skaters like Vanessa Torres and Lyn-z Adams Hawkins. Today, women compete in all major skateboarding events, such as the Gravity Games, the X Games, and the Slam City Jam. The Gravity Games offered medals to competing women for the first time in 2004. The X Games began offering women medals in 2002. Torres was the first

Here, Cara-Beth Burnside performs a melon air during a women's bowl competition in the Vans Triple Crown. Burnside is one of the pioneers of female skateboarding.

female skater to receive a gold medal at the X Games. She is one of the best female skaters today and is known for her charismatic personality. Torres is also featured in the Tony Hawk video game *Proving Ground*. Lyn-z Adams Hawkins started competing young. She won her first gold medal in women's vert at the 2004 X Games. She now has many medals under her belt. There have been two major skate films featuring women: *Getting Nowhere Faster* and *AKA: Girl Skater*.

Going Mainstream

In the past, skateboarders were considered to be rebellious and non-conformist. This image has faded in recent years. Two very different views of skaters exist today. Magazines like *Thrasher* still portray skateboarders as rebellious, dirty, and firmly connected to punk. However, other magazines like *Transworld Skateboarding* paint a different picture. These magazines portray skateboarding as modern and diverse. They portray skateboarding stars as controlled athletes. The trends in skateboarding, along with the dedication, professionalism, and skill of today's skaters, have led to the acceptance of skateboarding in mainstream America. Today, skateboarding is considered by most to be a real sport. It has become something that many American families enjoy doing or watching together.

Backside Air

1. Ride up the transition.
2. Grab the board on the heel side with your front hand.
3. Lift off.
4. Turn backside (toward your toes).
5. Keep your momentum going in a carving line and your board under you.
6. Land forward and skate away.

1

6

3

4

5

6

GLOSSARY

deck The main part of the skateboard that the rider stands on.

extreme action sports Sports that are seen as having a high level of energy and danger; also called action sports.

forward-to-fakie indy 720 A trick that involves spinning 720 degrees and landing backward.

heelflip A trick that involves spinning the skateboard with the heel of the foot while in the air.

kickflip A trick where the skateboard turns side-over-side under the skater.

kickflip 540 A trick where the skateboard turns 540 degrees side-over-side under the skater.

motocross Motorcycle racing that involves going over steep hills and sharp curves.

ollie 540 A trick done by popping the skateboard into the air and spinning 540 degrees before landing.

ollie impossible A trick where the skater jumps into the air, gets the board to flip end-over-end around the back foot, and then lands on the board.

punk A youth movement characterized by loud, aggressive music and confrontational attitudes.

varial 720 A trick that involves jumping up, rotating 720 degrees, and landing with the feet opposite to where they began.

vert skating The type of skating where the rider flies up into the air with the use of ramps.

X Games An annual sporting competition that focuses on extreme action sports.

FOR MORE INFORMATION

Action Sports Alliance
150 Research Drive
Hampton, VA 23666
(757) 810-3935
Web site: http://www.actionsportsalliance.com
The Alliance is a nonprofit association of professional women skateboarders and
other sports athletes. Its goal is to encourage young women's participation in
sports and to increase professional opportunities for women.

California Amateur Skateboard League (CASL)
P.O. Box 30004
San Bernadino, CA 92413
(909) 883-6176
Web site: http://www.caslusf.com
The California Amateur Skateboard League is organized by the United Skateboard
Federation, Inc. It has contests in both Northern and Southern California.

International Association of Skateboard Companies (IASC)
22431 Antonio Parkway, Suite B160-412
Rancho Santa Margarita, CA 92688
(949) 455-1112
Web site: http://www.skateboardiasc.org
The International Association of Skateboard Companies is a nonprofit organization that
was formed in 1995. Its mission is to increase participation in skateboarding,
educate young people about skateboarding, and be a resource on the skateboarding industry.

Skatelab

4226 Valley Fair Street

Simi Valley, CA 93063

Web site: http://www.skatelab.com

Skatelab is an indoor skatepark and museum. It serves to educate people about skateboarding.

United Skateboarding Association (USA)

40 West 23rd Street

New York, NY 10010

(732) 432-5400

Web site: http://www.unitedskate.com

The United Skateboarding Association provides event listings, contest results, videos, and skateboard links.

Web Sites

Due to the changing nature of Internet links, Rosen Publishing has developed an online list of Web sites related to the subject of this book. This site is updated regularly. Please use this link to access the list:

http://www.rosenlinks.com/ssk/stt

Bermudez, Ian. *Skate! The Mongo's Guide to Skateboarding.* New York, NY: Cheapskate Press, 2001.

Burke, L. M. *Skateboarding! Surf the Pavement.* New York, NY: Rosen Publishing Group, Inc., 1999.

Hawk, Tony. *Tony Hawk: Professional Skateboarder.* New York, NY: HarperCollins Publishers, Inc., 2002.

Herran, Joe, and Ron Thomas. *Skateboarding.* Philadelphia, PA: Chelsea House, 2003.

Hocking, Justin. *Rippin' Ramps: A Skateboarder's Guide to Riding Half-Pipes.* New York, NY: Rosen Publishing Group, Inc., 2005.

Murdico, Suzanne J. *Skateboarding in the X Games* (The World of Skateboarding). New York, NY: Rosen Publishing Group, Inc., 2003.

Powell, Ben. *Skateboarding.* Minneapolis, MN: Lerner, 2004.

Savage, Jeff. *Tony Hawk: Skateboarding Legend.* Mankato, MN: Edge Books, 2005.

Werner, Doug. *Skateboarder's Start-Up: A Beginner's Guide to Skateboarding.* San Diego, CA: Tracks Publishing, 2000.

Wingate, Brian. *The Complete Book of Skateboarding and Skateboarding Gear* (The World of Skateboarding). New York, NY: Rosen Publishing Group, Inc., 2003.

BIBLIOGRAPHY

AST.com. "AST Dew Tour: Tour Overview." NBC Sports, 2007. Retrieved April 2008 (http://www.ast.com/modules.php?name=Content&pa=showpage&pid=172).

Crossingham, John. *Skateboarding in Action*. New York, NY: Crabtree Publishing Company, 2002.

Davis, James. *Skateboarding Is Not a Crime: 50 Years of Street Culture*. Buffalo, NY: Firefly Books, 2004.

Detrick, Ben. "Skateboarding Rolls Out of the Suburbs." *New York Times*, November 11, 2007. Retrieved April 4, 2008 (http://www.nytimes.com/2007/11/11/fashion/11skaters.html?_r=2&partner=rssnyt&emc=rss&oref=slogin&oref=slogin).

Fenton, Mary. "The Death of Vert." EXPN.com, April 4, 2008. Retrieved April 4, 2008 (http://expn.go.com/expn/story?id=3327593#).

Goodfellow, Evan. *Skateboarding: Endless Grinds and Slides*. San Diego, CA: Tracks Publishing, 2005.

Goodfellow, Evan. *Skateboarding: Ramp Tricks*. San Diego, CA: Tracks Publishing, 2006.

Loizos, Constance. *Skateboard!: Your Guide to Street, Vert, Downhill, and More*. Washington, D.C.: National Geographic, 2002.

Miclaus, Claudia. "Skateboarding: A Sport? A Life Style? Or the Birth of a Trend?" Buzzle.com, April 7, 2007. Retrieved April 4, 2008 (http://www.buzzle.com/articles/skateboarding-sport-life-style-birth-trend.html).

Preszler, Eric. *Skateboarding*. Mankato, MN: Capstone Press, 2005.

RodneyMullen.net. "Rodney Mullen Biography." Retrieved April 4, 2008 (http://www.rodneymullen.net/bio/).

Savage, Jeff. *Street Skating: Grinds and Grabs*. Mankato, MN: Capstone Press, 2005.

Stricker, Eric. "Pro Spotlight: Daewon Song." *Transworld Skateboarding*, February 4, 2004. Retrieved April 2008 (http://www.skateboarding.com/skate/magazine/article/0,23271,594248,00.html).

TonyHawk.com. "Tony Hawk Bio." 2005. Retrieved April 4, 2008 (http://www.tonyhawk.com/bio.html).

Zolum.com. "Skateboarding Trick Guide." September 8, 2006. Retrieved April 4, 2008 (http://www.zolum.com/xsports/skate/73/skateboarding-trick-guide).

INDEX

About the Author

Heather Hasan has always been a sports enthusiast, no matter what the sport. Throughout her life, she has played softball, soccer, field hockey, and lacrosse. She also swam competitively, skied, and snowboarded. She currently lives in Pennsylvania with her husband, Omar, and their sons, Samuel and Matthew.

Photo Credits

Designer: Nelson Sá; Editor: Nicholas Croce
Photo Researcher: Amy Feinberg